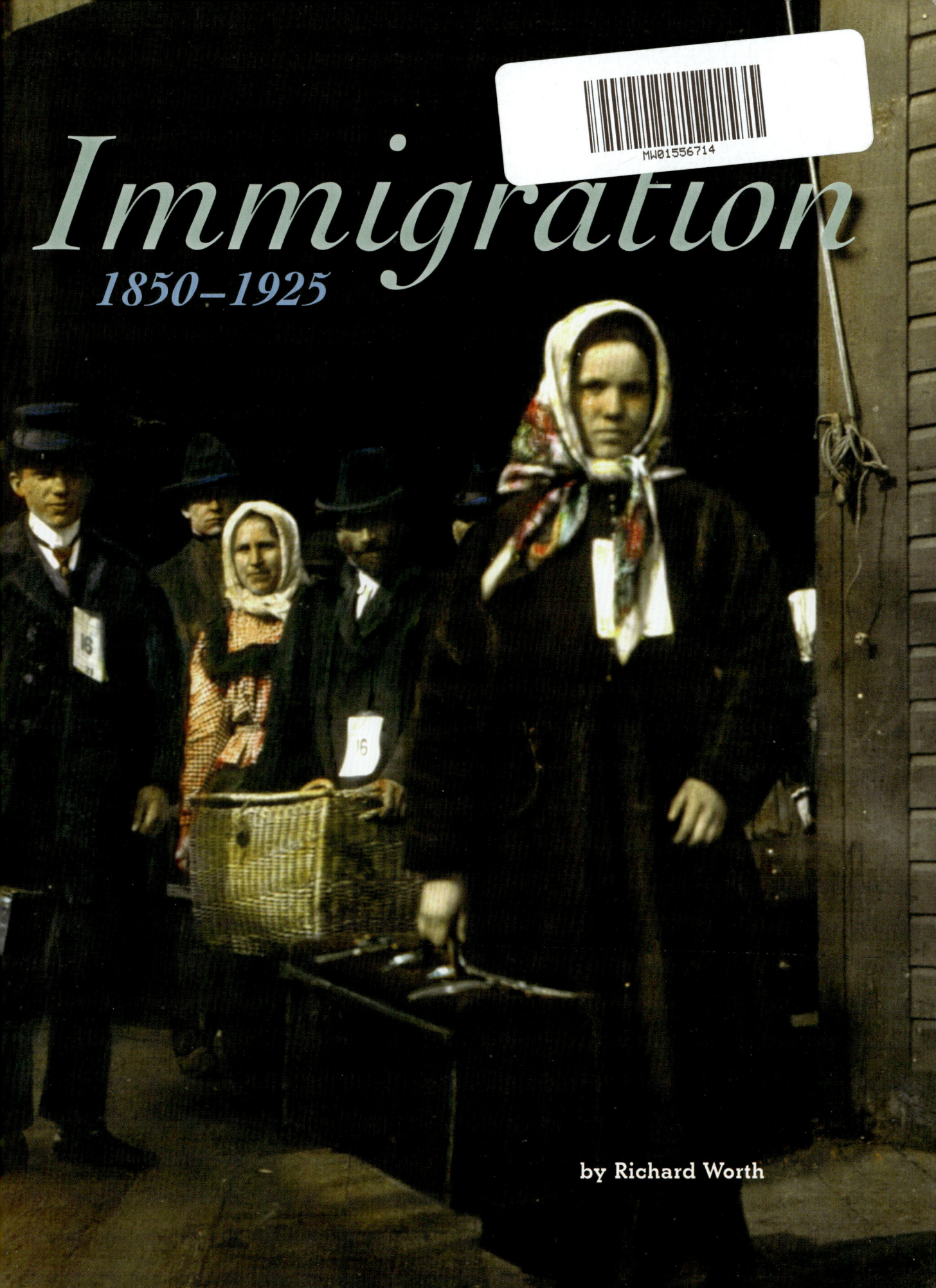

Immigration
1850–1925

by Richard Worth

What brought immigrants to the United States between 1850 and 1925 and what was their lasting impact on the nation?

Table of Contents

INTRODUCTION
A Picture Is Worth a Thousand Words 4
The United States experienced major waves of immigration between 1880 and 1930. Many personal accounts of this time have been captured in famous photographs that highlight the diversity of a great nation.

CHAPTER 1
Push and Pull Factors 6
What factors persuaded immigrants to come to the United States during the 19th and early 20th centuries?

CHAPTER 2
European Immigrants 16
Why did European immigrants come to the United States during the 19th and early 20th centuries?

Cartoonist's Notebook 28

CHAPTER 3
Asian and Mexican Immigrants 30
Why did Asian and Mexican immigrants come to the United States during the 19th and early 20th centuries?

Conclusion: The Great Mosaic 42
How to Write a Biography 44
Glossary 46
Index 48

{ Introduction }

A Picture Is Worth a Thousand Words

▲ A colorized photograph of immigrants arriving in the United States at Ellis Island, taken by Lewis Hine.

In 1892, Ellis Island became an immigrant station for people from Europe who wanted to live in the United States. Ellis Island lies in New York Harbor, near the Statue of Liberty. "Lady Liberty," as she is called, was among the first sights that immigrants saw as they approached the United States. After the ship on which they were traveling dropped anchor, the immigrants were directed to the Ellis Island inspection station.

Frequently, entire families made the journey together from Europe, carrying their belongings in only one or two suitcases. Immigration officials from the U.S. Bureau of Immigration asked them questions. What were their names? What country did they come from? Then, if they passed a physical examination conducted by doctors at the immigration center, the immigrants were allowed to enter the United States.

In 1904, Lewis Hine—a New York City teacher and amateur photographer—began photographing immigrants at Ellis Island. He taught at a school for children of immigrants. He took the photographs, in part, to help his students feel pride in the common heritage they shared with these newly arriving immigrant families. Though his equipment was heavy and cumbersome, and it could take hours to set up a shot, he managed to persuade individuals and families to pose for him and help him wrestle his camera and tripod into position.

The result was a series of portraits in black and white that captured the dreams and anxieties of many immigrants as they arrived in America. Read on to learn more about the immigrant experience in the late 19th and early 20th centuries and how these people would come to shape the United States as we know it today.

▲ It is estimated that a total of twelve million immigrants passed through Ellis Island from 1892 until it closed in 1954. Roughly 40 percent of American citizens living today can trace at least one ancestor to Ellis Island. During its peak years from 1900 to 1910, Ellis Island processed anywhere from 5,000 to 10,000 people per day.

{ Chapter 1 }

Push and Pull Factors

What factors persuaded immigrants to come to the United States during the 19th and early 20th centuries?

▲ Many immigrants were poor and traveled in crowded conditions aboard ships.

ESSENTIAL VOCABULARY

- anti-Semitism   page 13
- census   page 7
- emigrate   page 8
- ghetto   page 12
- immigrate   page 7
- indentured servant page 8
- pull factor   page 8
- push factor   page 8
- tsar   page 13

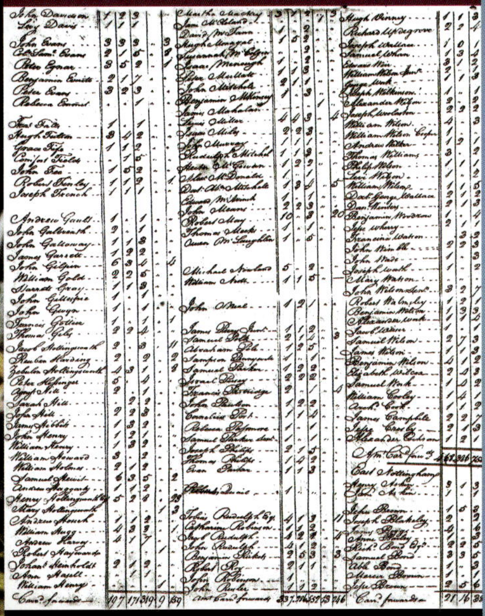

▲ The first U.S. Census was taken in 1790.

At the time of the first official United States **census** in 1790, there were fewer than four million residents in the United States, including all free and enslaved persons. By 1820, that number had almost doubled, but the population was still less than ten million. With the exception of Native Americans, most free Americans at this time were the descendants of European colonists who had settled the first English, Dutch, and French colonies during the 1600s and 1700s.

At that time, fewer than ten thousand people willfully **immigrated** to America each year on average. By 1920, the average annual number of immigrants entering the United States had exploded to more than one million—fifty times greater than the number just a century earlier. What brought about this explosive growth in immigration? There were many different factors that caused people from Europe, Asia, and Latin America to move to the United States during this period, and the impact of the massive immigration from 1850 to 1925 would be felt in every state, and ultimately reshape the nation.

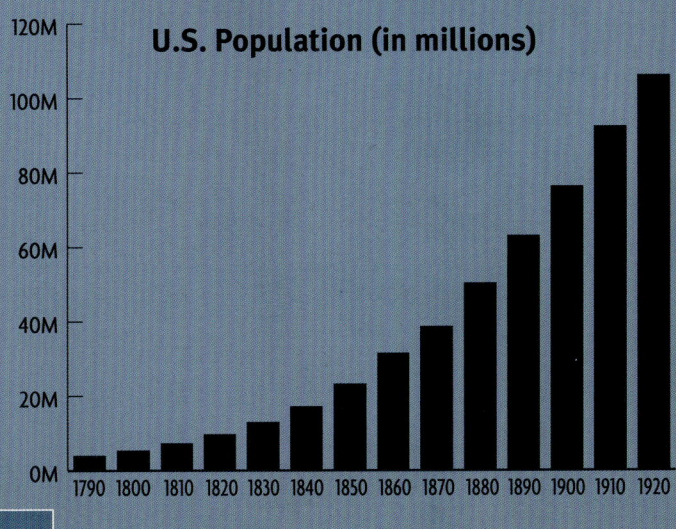

U.S. Population (in millions)

{ Chapter 1 }

▲ This painting depicts the arrival of immigrants in the port of New York.

Reasons for Immigration

Historians have identified a variety of reasons why people **emigrate** from their country of birth and start over in a new place. Leaving one's homeland is not an easy thing to do—especially if people reside in a place their ancestors have inhabited for many generations. Immigrating to a new country to make a new home and carve out a new life is a difficult task, rife with fear and anxiety. The motivating forces that cause people to leave must be strong. Historians call these forces push and pull factors. **Push factors** are events or circumstances that push populations out of their current home. **Pull factors** are events or opportunities that pull populations toward the possibilities of better circumstances.

As early as the 1600s, for example, people of the struggling lower classes left Europe and went to the British colonies in North America as **indentured servants**, hoping to find a better life. These people could not afford to pay the price of passage to the New World, so in return for passage as well as a place to live and food to eat in the new colony, the indentured servants agreed to work without wages. The voyage was very difficult, and passengers were given small amounts of bread that were supposed to last them for two weeks. If they ran out, they would starve. Some did perish on the voyage. After arriving in North America, some worked in towns, while others tilled the land for large landowners. The term of the indenture was usually four to seven years. At the end, the new immigrants received their freedom and some land to farm. The promise of land and a chance to climb out of poverty pulled them toward the United States.

Push and Pull Factors

Forced Migration

Many immigrants chose to leave their homelands and live in another country. But some people in history have been forced to relocate against their will. Between 1600 and 1865 an estimated 12.5 million Africans were taken captive by enemy tribes, traded, and sold into slavery in the Americas.

The captives were typically abducted in raids by warring tribes in the African interior and then transported to the West African coast by African traders. There, they were jailed at trading posts, branded with a hot iron, and sold to European slave traders who transported the Africans aboard cargo ships bound for the American colonies.

The slaves were chained together, and hundreds were packed below decks for the journey across the Atlantic Ocean. Aboard ship, many died from lack of food and water or from disease. The voyage across the Atlantic could last as long as three months, especially if the ship hit bad weather. The slaves who survived the voyage aboard the slave ships were sold in South America, the Caribbean islands, and North America. Many then spent the rest of their lives working on plantations that grew crops such as sugarcane, rice, cotton, and tobacco.

By 1860, there were four million enslaved African Americans living in the American South. These men, women, and children were emancipated in 1865 with the ratification of the Thirteenth Amendment to the Constitution, which abolished slavery in the United States.

▼ After emancipation, thousands of freed men and women left the rural South and migrated to urban areas in the North.

▼ Beginning in the 1500s, Africans were sold into slavery and shipped to the American colonies. Hundreds of thousands of Africans became part of the slave trade to British North America.

{ Chapter 1 }

In the 1800s, people in Ireland and Germany experienced terrible hardships. In Ireland, during the 1840s, a fungus infected potato plants, causing the region's primary crop to fail. These crop failures, along with harsh policies by the ruling British government, led to a devastating food shortage in which hundreds of thousands of poor Irish starved to death. The Great Potato Famine, or Great Hunger, caused many Irish nationals to emigrate in search of food and jobs. More than two million people—half of the population of Ireland at the time—left and relocated in North America. At the same time, major unemployment and social and political unrest that culminated in a revolution in Germany led millions of Germans to emigrate. These events caused more than five million Irish and German immigrants to make the passage to America between 1820 and 1870. The Great Hunger in Ireland and the revolution in Germany were both push factors that forced many people to move and seek a new life in a new land.

▼ The Great Hunger of 1846–1847 led to massive emigration from Ireland and the arrival of millions of Irish immigrants in America.

In January 1848, while Ireland was being decimated by famine and Germany was heading toward revolutionary upheaval, gold was discovered near Sacramento, California.

The Gold Rush that followed, beginning in 1849, would be another major pull factor, not only luring thousands of American settlers westward, but also drawing thousands of Chinese prospectors eastward, across the Pacific Ocean to the California Coast. In 1852 alone, more than twenty thousand Chinese immigrants came on a quest for gold.

▲ The California Gold Rush drew prospectors from all over the world. Many thousands of Chinese immigrants came seeking their fortune.

Historical Perspective

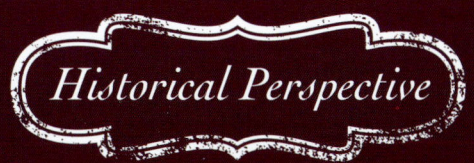

Centuries of Immigration

The waves of immigration that brought so many people to the United States in the mid-1800s and early 1900s were only the latest in a vast flow that had been occurring for centuries. The earliest Native American cultures descended from the indigenous peoples of Siberia who migrated across the Bering land bridge into North America more than ten thousand years ago, most likely looking for food.

Beginning in the 1500s, European explorers began arriving in North America. French sailors explored the St. Lawrence River and behind them came traders, priests, and settlers who immigrated to the area. They trapped beaver for their fur, which was used to make hats and coats valued by Europeans. They also came to farm the land and grow wheat. Southward, during the 1600s, English colonists immigrated to North America. They began to set up settlements in places like Virginia and Massachusetts. Some came seeking gold, some sought land and other natural resources, and others sought the freedom to practice their religion without persecution.

World Migration

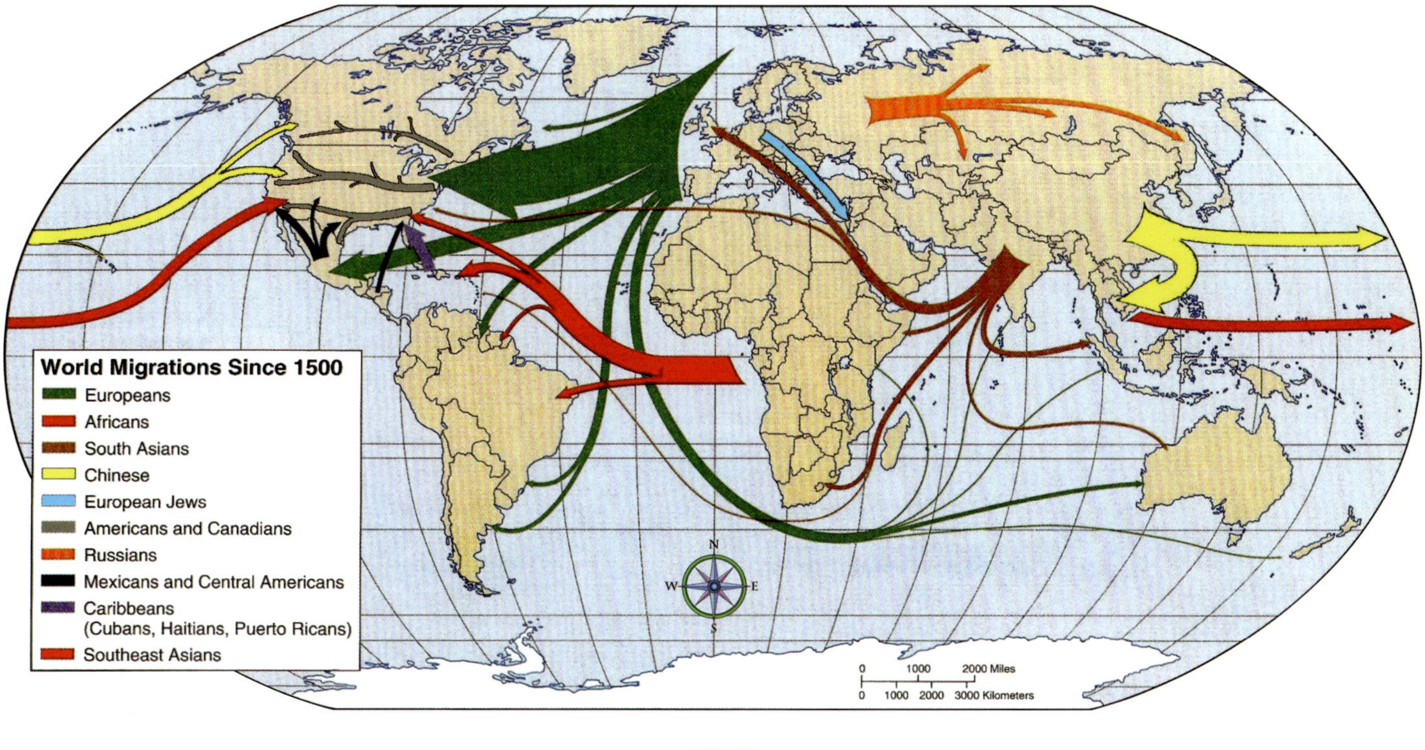
World Migrations Since 1500
Europeans
Africans
South Asians
Chinese
European Jews
Americans and Canadians
Russians
Mexicans and Central Americans
Caribbeans
(Cubans, Haitians, Puerto Ricans)
Southeast Asians
N
S
E
W
0 1000 2000 Miles
0 1000 2000 3000 Kilometers

{ Chapter 1 }

Prior to the mid-1800s, most immigrants who came to North America by choice hailed from Northern and Western Europe. Many, with the exception of the Irish Catholics, were Protestant and literate. While many Irish were impoverished, some Germans possessed enough financial stability to be able to make it to the Midwest to purchase and settle farmland. Most Irish, on the other hand, could not afford to buy land, and they settled in the urban areas of the Northeast, becoming part of the growing industrial workforce.

Soon economic hardship, social and political instability, and religious persecution would drive millions of Southern and Eastern Europeans across the Atlantic. Catholic, Eastern Orthodox, and Jewish immigrants from countries like Croatia, Greece, Italy, Poland, Russia, Serbia, and Slovakia flooded in. Unlike the Germans who had preceded them and who could afford to move to the Midwest and purchase land to settle and farm, these immigrants had very little money, so they crowded into cramped quarters in the northeastern port cities where they landed. Unskilled laborers found work in factories, where they worked long hours for little pay and often faced ethnic or religious discrimination.

For example, in the late 1800s, severe brutality and religious persecution in Russia pushed many people out of Eastern Europe and Russia to the east coast. Among these were many Jewish immigrants. Jewish people in Russia, for example, had faced religious discrimination for centuries. They were forced to live in **ghettos**, poor areas in Russian towns.

Poverty, discrimination, and the fear of violence pushed many Jewish people out of Russia. ▶

▲ Poverty and political violence are powerful push factors causing immigration.

Science and Anthropology

Behavioral Adaptations

Like all animals, human beings have become adapted to their environment over time. Some of these adaptations are physical and others are behavioral. For example, living together in groups and migrating are both examples of behavioral adaptations that humans have adapted to survive.

During the 19th century, Jews also faced violent attacks by the Russian government, which believed they were plotting against the **tsar**—the Russian ruler. Beginning in the 1880s, many Jewish families began leaving Russia and immigrating to the United States. Though they sought freedom from religious persecution, there were many Americans who were not accepting of Jews, who often suffered rampant **anti-Semitism** in the United States.

Religious discrimination, such as that experienced by Irish Catholics, German Lutherans, and Jews, was an important factor that pushed immigrants out of Europe. Just as the promise of religious tolerance pulled settlers to Pennsylvania in the 1600s, it pulled these groups to the United States in the 1800s and 1900s.

Another factor that spurred immigration was political freedom. In the late 19th century, Mexico was ruled by a brutal dictator with absolute power over the military and government. Mexicans who spoke out against the government were condemned to death, and therefore many Mexican nationals were forced to flee to the United States, where freedom of speech was guaranteed by the U.S. Constitution. Eventually, a civil war broke out in Mexico. Political violence frightened many Mexicans, who then also left their homeland for the United States. Poverty and low wages in Mexico were another factor that drove Mexicans northward to find better-paying jobs.

{ Chapter 1 }

Push and pull factors frequently act together, causing the powerful forces behind immigration. Political violence can be a push factor, while political freedom is a pull factor. Poverty pushes people out of their homeland, while an opportunity to find a job pulls them to a new city in the United States.

Checkpoint
Read More About It

In the United States, the U.S. Constitution guarantees religious freedom. Go online or visit your local library to read more about the discrimination faced by Europeans. Learn how this compared to what they experienced as immigrants in the United States.

As the 19th century came to a close, the number of immigrants coming to the United States had risen from about ten thousand per year to about one million. People of increasingly diverse economic, social, and cultural backgrounds would come seeking new lives for their families. These people would quickly be absorbed into the American workforce, carving out areas such as Chinatown, Greektown, Little Germany, and Little Italy in America's cities, a patchwork of cultures forming the fabric of a new nation.

▼ As a result of many push and pull factors, immigration to America exploded between 1850 and 1920, allowing for a rich mosaic of cultures, languages, and religions to thrive.

Summing Up

- Push and pull factors are the forces behind immigration and migration.

- Push factors can be rooted in economics, such as poverty, hunger, low wages, or unaffordable living conditions.

- Push factors can also be rooted in human rights and ideology, such as the desire to escape injustice or discrimination.

- Pull factors are often rooted in the possibility of new and better economic opportunities and safety, such as pursuit of wealth, better living conditions, or pursuit of religious or political freedom.

- A combination of these factors led to massive immigrations from Europe, Mexico, and Asia between 1850 and 1920.

Putting It All Together

Choose one of the following research activities. Work independently, in pairs, or in small groups. Share your responses with your class, and listen to others present their work.

1. Research the ships and the slave captains that brought slaves to the Americas. Write a biography of someone from this period who made the passage aboard one of these ships.

2. Immigrants brought words from the language of their homelands to America. The words have become part of our English vernacular. For example, **jazz** has African origins, **stoop** is a Dutch word, and **schmooze** is Hebrew. Look up the country of origin for the following words: **noodle, delicatessen, barbecue, patio, cookie, sled, opera,** and **phony**. Write the words and define their meaning.

3. Study photographs taken by Lewis Hine at Ellis Island from 1904 to 1909. Select one person from a photo and thoroughly examine the image. After studying the person's face, write a monologue from his or her point of view. What is the person thinking at that point in life? Draw on information from this chapter.

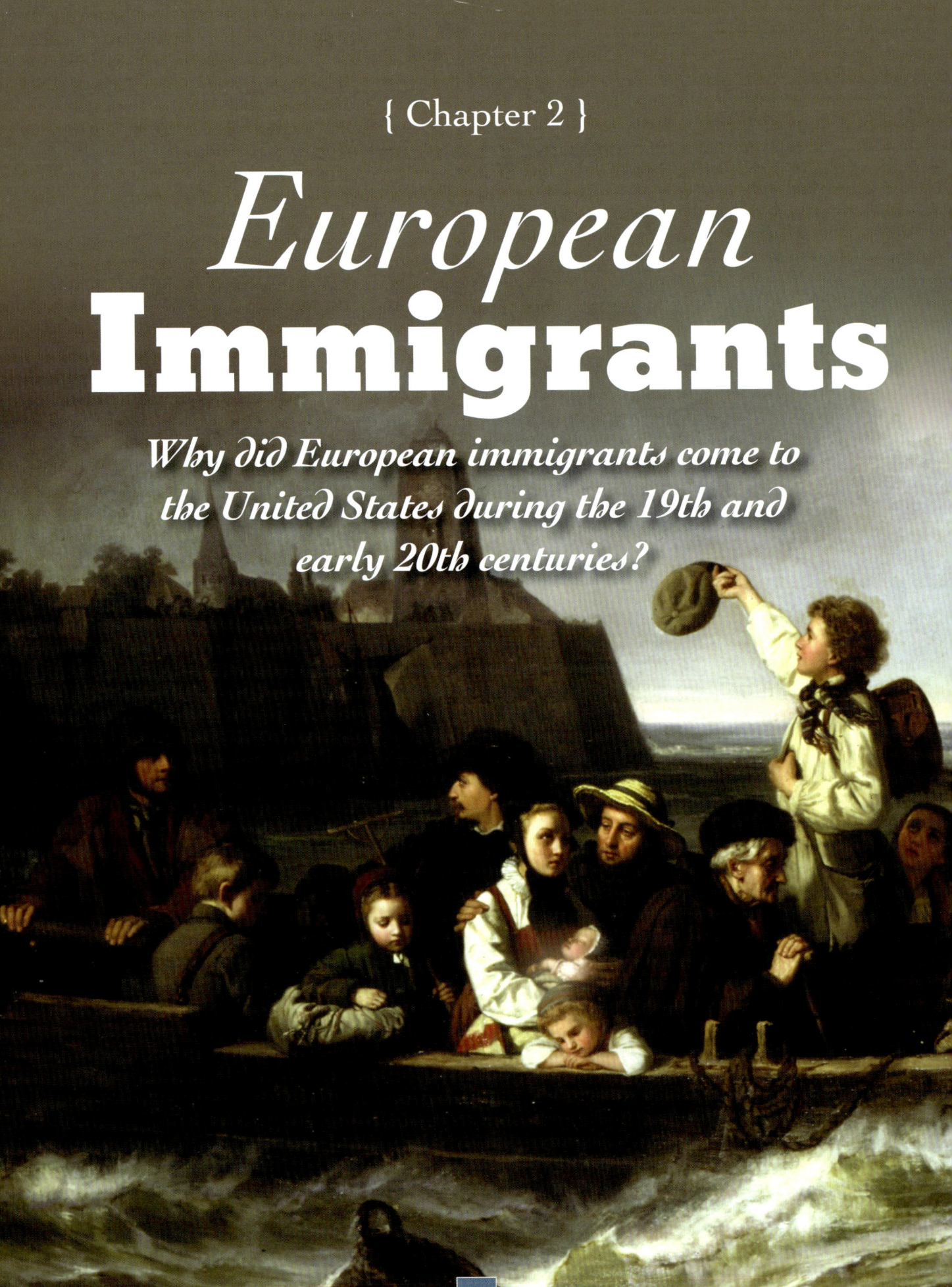

{ Chapter 2 }

European Immigrants

Why did European immigrants come to the United States during the 19th and early 20th centuries?

ESSENTIAL VOCABULARY

- intolerance — page 20
- pogrom — page 20
- sweatshop — page 23

▲ Famine and political unrest caused millions of Irish and Germans to immigrate to America beginning in the 1850s.

Between 1880 and 1930, more than twenty million people left their homeland and immigrated to the United States. Most were Europeans forced from their distinctive homelands by various factors and drawn to America because it was considered a land of promise. The first wave of European immigrants began with Irish, German, British, Scandinavian, and other Northern European immigrants in the mid-1800s. The second wave began in the 1890s with Italian, Jewish, Slavic, and other Southeastern European immigrants.

The Irish Migration

The overwhelming majority of the Irish who began coming in the 1850s after the Great Hunger could not afford to buy land. Most were poor and came seeking work and better living conditions. They often traveled from Ireland to Liverpool, England, where they boarded a ship bound for America. They spent several weeks at sea, traveling in steerage, below decks. They were crowded together in hot, dusty conditions, where many of them suffered from seasickness.

Without any savings, arriving in port cities such as Boston and New York, many could not afford to venture west and take advantage of the vast unclaimed territories. However, the Irish had a strong work ethic and many quickly found work in the Northeastern industrial corridor, where they ran machinery in textile mills and other types of factories. They also became the largest force of manual laborers.

{ Chapter 2 }

The Irish who came to America not only benefited from the living and working conditions in the states, they also made major contributions to American culture and infrastructure. In time, they became political and religious leaders. They excelled in journalism, entertainment, and sports. Irish laborers helped build the railroads, canals, and bridges, and played a large role in mining as well. New York's Erie Canal was dug by five thousand Irish laborers in the 1820s. The Brooklyn Bridge, completed in 1883, was also built by a predominantly Irish American workforce. They also established the first labor unions in the country during the 1800s in order to negotiate with big businesses and improve working conditions and wages.

Though they faced discrimination and challenges assimilating because of their Catholic religion, they managed to become very much a part of the mainstream culture, while still retaining pride in their heritage.

▲ The Irish made major contributions to the building of America's infrastructure.

Primary Source

A Letter to the Editor

Not all who ventured to America were destitute. This letter to the editor ran in the *London Times* in 1850. Though the author's name is unknown, it appears to have been written by a wealthy Irish immigrant to America.

"I am exceedingly well pleased at coming to this land of plenty. On arrival I purchased 120 acres of land at $5 an acre. You must bear in mind that I have purchased the land out, and it is to me and mine an "estate for ever", without a landlord, an agent or tax-gatherer to trouble me. I would advise all my friends to quit Ireland—the country most dear to me; as long as they remain in it they will be in bondage and misery.

What you labour for is sweetened by contentment and happiness; there is no failure in the potato crop, and you can grow every crop you wish, without manuring the land during life. You need not mind feeding pigs, but let them into the woods and they will feed themselves, until you want to make bacon of them.

I shudder when I think that starvation prevails to such an extent in poor Ireland. After supplying the entire population of America, there would still be as much corn and provisions left as would supply the world, for there is no limit to cultivation or end to land. Here the meanest labourer has beef and mutton, with bread, bacon, tea, coffee, sugar and even pies, the whole year round …."

The German Migration

Just as the threat of starvation drove the Irish to America's shores, the March Revolution, which took place in the German states in 1848, drove many German immigrants to the United States. The Germans who fled sought financial and political stability. Many were literate, had a strong work ethic, and felt a deep commitment to education. Many also had enough wealth that they could afford to move west once they arrived in the United States.

They Made a Difference

Early Education

German immigrants in Wisconsin introduced the concept of kindergarten to the United States, offering education to young children. The word **kindergarten** literally means "children's garden" in German. The term was coined by German educator Friedrich Fröbel in reference to his method of developing intelligence in young children. German immigrants also popularized the idea of gymnasiums, athletic centers, and public schools.

As a result, many German immigrants became homesteaders who moved to the Midwest to work, settle American territories, raise families, and establish farms and ranches.

During the 19th century, with the advancements of the Industrial Revolution, Europe made a sharp transformation from a continent of largely rural and agrarian states to a highly industrialized region. As a result of industrialization, overpopulation, and urbanization, many nations suffered great political and social upheaval. Beginning in the 1890s, millions of Italians, Slavs, and Jews immigrated to the United States.

The Italian Migration

Between 1890 and 1915, more than four million Italians immigrated to America, most from Southern Italy. Some were skilled craftsmen, who were literate and had high ranking as carpenters, masons, tailors, and barbers. Others had worked in textile factories in Piedmont and Tuscany or the mines in Umbria and Sicily, but the majority were farm hands or unskilled manual laborers without much experience in industry. Nonetheless, they would soon become vital contributors to the U.S. labor force, leading workers in the mining, textile, and clothing-manufacturing industries.

◀ German farmers helped establish the Midwest as America's "breadbasket."

{ Chapter 2 }

The Jewish Migration

One of the first groups to suffer in these nations were Jews, who faced **intolerance** and were largely discriminated against because of their religion, even in times of peace and plenty.

Jews faced anti-Semitism across much of Europe. In some areas, they were not permitted to own land and in many cases they could not practice their religion. To escape these conditions, they had begun immigrating to North America. Jewish people from Central Europe had begun coming over to America in large numbers as early as the 1600s. Over time, civic unrest and discrimination against Jews persisted in Europe. To escape anti-Semitism and seek better living conditions and economic opportunities, more and more Jews began making the passage. In 1820, approximately three thousand Jews immigrated to America per year. By 1880, that number had multiplied by 100 with an average of three hundred thousand annually.

Then, in 1881, the Russian king, Tsar Alexander II, was assassinated. Many Russians thought Jews had been involved in the assassination. Because of their religion, they were targets of hatred by the Russian government and most Christian Russians.

Tsar Alexander II

The assassination prompted an even deeper persecution of Jews. Russian Jews regularly became the victims of **pogroms.** These were organized massacres of Jews by Christians. During pogroms, Jews were killed, their shops were destroyed, and their homes were burned. As a result, a large number of Jews fled Russia and immigrated to North America. Between 1881 and 1920, more than two and a half million Russian and Eastern European Jews immigrated to the United States. They settled in urban areas and joined the American working class. Many Russian Jews traveled by land from the Pale of Settlement to Germany, then by ship to Great Britain. There, they boarded another ship to cross the Atlantic Ocean.

▼ Two and a half million Jews fled Eastern Europe and Russia between 1881 and 1924.

The Root of the Meaning

Anti-Semitism comes from the combining of the Greek prefix *anti-*, which means "opposite," "opposed to," and the French word *Semite*, which refers to any culture with a Semitic language, such as Hebrew, Arabic, Assyrian, or Aramaean.

European Immigrants

The Pale of Jewish Settlement 1772–1917

▲ Jews in Russia were restricted to a territory known as the Pale of Settlement.

Once in America, Jews thrived in the urban centers of the Northeast. Literate, hardworking, and devoted to family and education, many Jewish men and women found jobs as skilled laborers, working in the garment industry, or opened small businesses. In 1880, more than eighty thousand Jews lived in New York. By 1924, that number had grown to two million, making it one quarter of the city's population. The period of large-scale Jewish immigration ended with restrictive immigration laws against Jews and other minorities that were passed in 1921 and 1924. However, their vast contributions to American industry, education, the arts, and culture continue to resonate today.

History and Literature

Emma Lazarus (1849–1887)

Those immigrants who came ashore at Ellis Island could see the Statue of Liberty in the harbor. At its base were inscribed words that had been written by Jewish poet Emma Lazarus.

"Give me your tired, your poor,
Your huddled masses yearning to breathe free."

Emma Lazarus was born in New York City in 1849. She came from a well-to-do Jewish family. She wrote several books of poems, including *Admetus and Other Poems*, published in 1871, and *The Spagnoletto*, published in 1876. One of her most famous books of poetry was *Songs of a Semite*, published in 1882. Lazarus was inspired by her outrage over the pogroms in Russia. The words from her poem "The New Colossus," about the Statue of Liberty, were engraved on the statue.

{ Chapter 2 }

Life in Urban Centers

Jews were just one part of a large migration of Southern and Eastern Europeans who came to the United States between 1880 and 1930. During this period, more than twenty million Irish, Italians, Russians, Germans, Poles, Hungarians, and Serbians arrived. More than two million Canadians and one million Swedes also immigrated to America.

Most of the Europeans who came to the United States were poor and had barely been able to scrape together the $34 boat fare to travel to America. What awaited them was something better than the lives they had known in Europe. Many settled in urban enclaves such as New York's Lower East Side.

In 1890, Jacob Riis, a Danish immigrant and journalist, published *How the Other Half Lives*, about conditions among immigrants in New York City. In words and photographs he told of his own journey through tenements, the multistory buildings with many families crowded into dark, dirty rooms.

▲ Many Eastern Europeans lived in dark tenement buildings along the Lower East Side of New York.

"... two small rooms in a six-story tenement were made to hold a 'family' of father and mother, twelve children and six boarders." As Riis pointed out, many families both lived and worked in the same rooms. Some made clothes that were sold in New York City. Others made lace that was sewed onto pillows, while still others produced artificial flowers. "Every member of the family, from the youngest to the oldest, bears a hand, shut in the qualmy [dirty, hot] rooms, where meals are cooked and clothing washed and dried besides, the livelong day. It is not unusual to find a dozen persons—men, women, and children—at work in a single small room."

The tenement apartments were dark, often with no windows. There were no indoor toilets and no running water for the tenants to drink. Many children developed diseases such as measles and smallpox. Since they could not afford doctors or medicines, they often died from their illnesses.

Those Eastern Europeans who did not work in their apartments found work elsewhere. Some became peddlers, pushing carts full of secondhand clothes or other items through the Lower East Side. Others opened stores, and still others made a living as craftsmen—tailors, carpenters, and construction workers. Many, especially women, went to work in small factories known as **sweatshops.** In these places, they often worked eleven-hour days, six days a week, making clothing.

Working in a Sweatshop

One young immigrant named Sadie described working on a sewing machine in a clothing factory, where she earned about five dollars per week. "The machines go like mad all day, because the faster you work the more money you get. Sometimes in my haste I get my finger caught and the needle goes right through it. . . . I bind the finger up with a piece of cotton and go on working. . . . Where the needle goes through the nail it makes a sore finger, or where it splinters a bone it does much harm. Sometimes a finger has to come off."

▲ Women, men, and children worked long hours in hot, dusty sweatshops.

{ Chapter 2 }

Unions

Gradually workers began to gather together and form labor unions. The unions demanded better working conditions for their members. One of these was the International Ladies' Garment Workers' Union (ILGWU), formed in 1900. Many of the members were Jewish women who had recently immigrated to America and worked in the clothing industry. In 1909, approximately twenty thousand workers went out on strike in New York City, demanding higher wages and better working conditions. The majority were immigrant women who rallied around the slogan: "We'd rather starve quick than starve slow."

As a result of the strike, the women lost their jobs. Some were arrested and others were beaten up by thugs hired by factory owners to break up the strike. The strike was settled in 1910. Wages improved and working hours were shortened. An even larger strike the same year involved sixty thousand workers; they also won higher wages.

▼ During the Progressive Era, labor unions mobilized workers and helped them fight for higher wages and better working conditions.

Checkpoint
Make Connections

What labor unions are active in your community? Who do they serve? What strategies do they use to achieve their goals?

Some of the strikers had worked for the Triangle Shirtwaist Company located on Washington Place in lower Manhattan. When a fire broke out in the factory on March 25, 1911, women working in the factory were trapped, and many of the women were killed. The tragedy sparked an outcry for better, safer working conditions.

As a result of the fire in New York City, a committee was formed to investigate conditions at factories in the city. The New York Legislature also formed a commission. As a result, New York State began to reform its laws and improve working conditions.

While many immigrants made up the blue-collar labor force, immigrants also rose through the ranks, achieving economic success in a variety of areas. Some became bankers and store owners, while others became lawyers and doctors. Others achieved great fame in the arts and entertainment fields. No matter how much success immigrants and their children achieved, however, they still faced discrimination in the United States. Some people looked down on them because they had not been born in America. Others ridiculed those who had not mastered the English language.

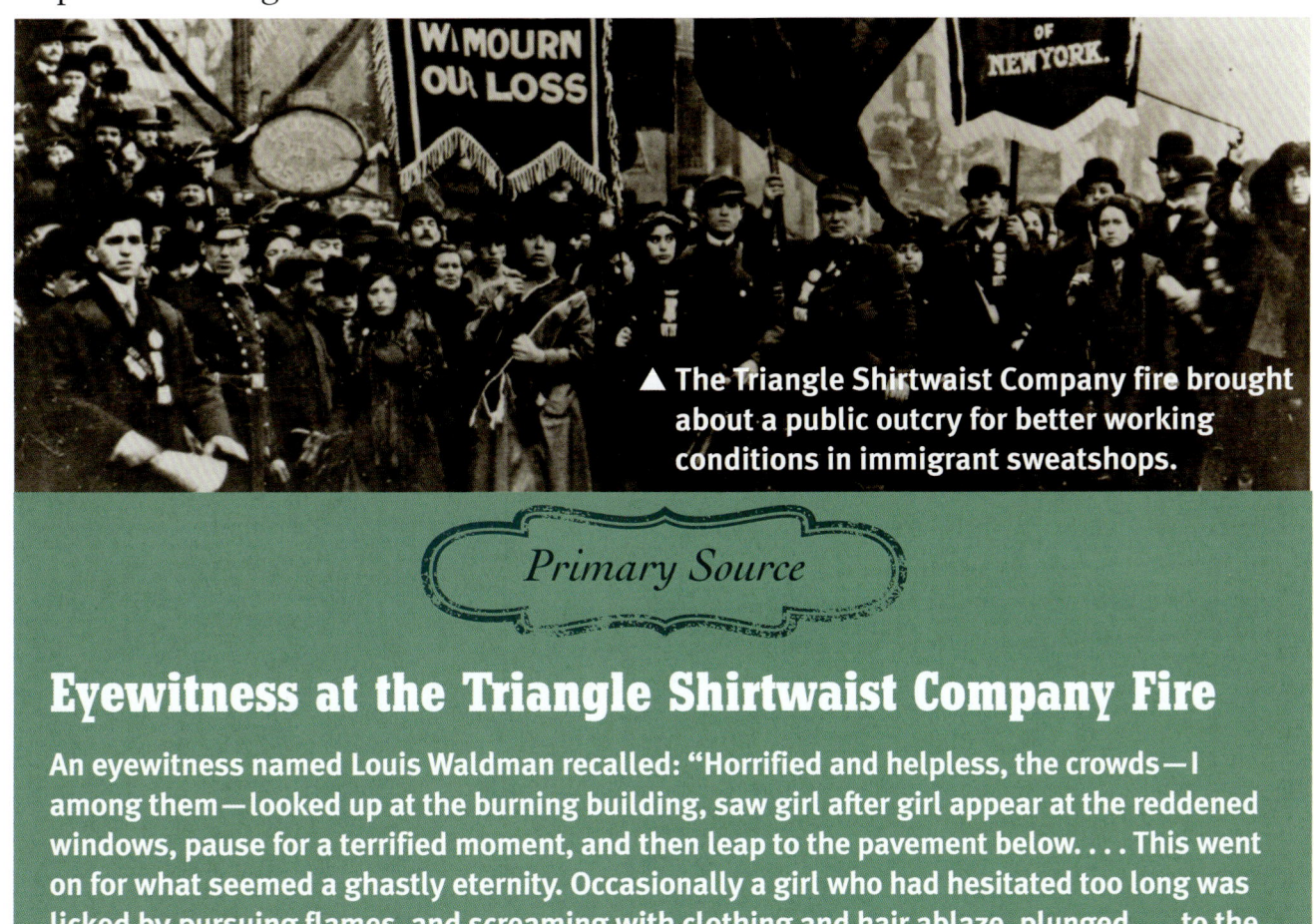

▲ The Triangle Shirtwaist Company fire brought about a public outcry for better working conditions in immigrant sweatshops.

Primary Source

Eyewitness at the Triangle Shirtwaist Company Fire

An eyewitness named Louis Waldman recalled: "Horrified and helpless, the crowds—I among them—looked up at the burning building, saw girl after girl appear at the reddened windows, pause for a terrified moment, and then leap to the pavement below. . . . This went on for what seemed a ghastly eternity. Occasionally a girl who had hesitated too long was licked by pursuing flames, and screaming with clothing and hair ablaze, plunged . . . to the street. Life nets held by the firemen were torn by the impact of the falling bodies."

{ Chapter 2 }

World War I and New Immigration Laws

In 1914, World War I broke out in Europe. The Allies—Britain, France, and Russia—fought against the Central Powers—Germany and Austria-Hungary. In 1917, following German attacks on American ships, President Woodrow Wilson declared war on the Central Powers. Many Eastern European immigrants enlisted in the U.S. Army to fight in Europe.

Also in 1917, the Russian tsar was overthrown and the Communists, led by Vladimir Ilyich Lenin, took power in Russia, which would become known as the Soviet Union in 1922. In America, some immigrants supported the communist government. Lenin made peace with the Central Powers in 1918, taking his country out of the war. Later that year the Allies, with the help of U.S. troops, finally defeated Germany and Austria-Hungary.

Following the end of World War I, attitudes toward immigration changed in the United States. The federal government feared that communism might spread to America. To combat this possibility, the U.S. Congress passed more restrictive immigration laws. During the 1920s, far fewer immigrants from Europe were permitted to enter the United States.

▲ Although World War I broke out in 1914, the United States did not declare war on the Central Powers until 1917.

Primary Source

First Amendment

"Congress shall make no law respecting an establishment of religion, or prohibiting the free exercise thereof; or abridging the freedom of speech, or of the press; or the right of the people peaceably to assemble, and to petition the Government for a redress of grievances."

European Immigrants

Summing Up

- Northern Europeans immigrated to the United States in large numbers between 1850 and 1880.

- Southern and Eastern Europeans immigrated to the United States in large numbers between 1880 and 1920.

- Many Jews came from Russia, trying to escape poverty, anti-Semitism, and pogroms. They were drawn to America by the promise of jobs and the freedom to practice their religion.

- Some of America's most famous business leaders and artists were immigrants, and from 1850, European immigrants changed the face of America.

Putting It All Together

Choose one of the following research activities. Work independently, in pairs, or in small groups. Share your responses with your class, and listen to others present their work.

1. Read about the social reformer Lillian Wald. Write a report about her contributions to American society.

2. Research firsthand accounts of working conditions in sweatshops of the late 19th century or early 20th century. Prepare a presentation to the class about them.

3. Use the Internet to find information about the International Ladies' Garment Workers' Union. Write a report about its early leaders and the role of the union in improving working conditions.

Optional Assignment: Assume you were living in America in 1911. Write a letter to the editor of a newspaper or conduct a role-play exercise protesting the deaths of 146 female garment workers in the Triangle Shirtwaist Company fire. Complain about the conditions in which they labored. Call for the start of specific government actions that address this tragedy and will prevent future ones from happening.

SERAFINA'S DILEMMA

CARTOONIST'S NOTEBOOK WRITTEN BY DENIS O'ROURKE AND HEIDI WARD
ILLUSTRATED BY ALEX CAÑAS

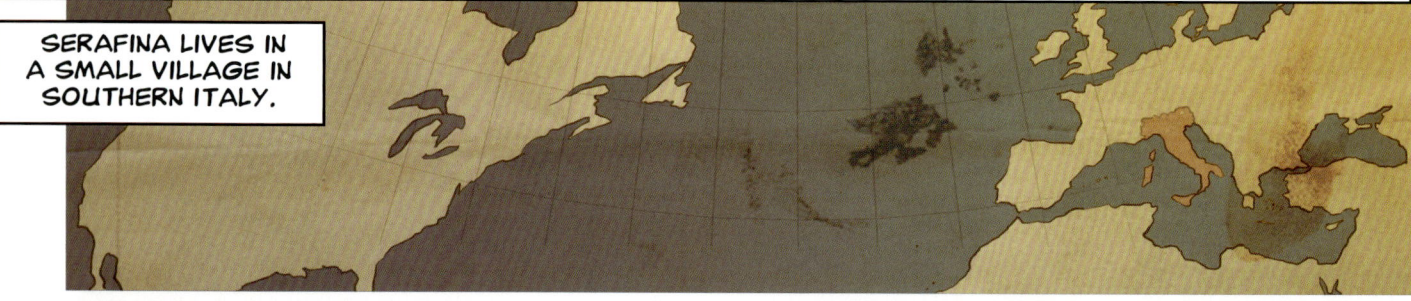

SERAFINA LIVES IN A SMALL VILLAGE IN SOUTHERN ITALY.

SERAFINA'S VILLAGE IS STRUGGLING DUE TO RECENT DROUGHTS.

I WANT US TO GO TO AMERICA, TO WORK AND SAVE MONEY.

MY DEAR ANTONIO, I HAVE HEARD STORIES OF PEOPLE LEAVING AND BEING UNABLE TO FIND WORK. MANY NEVER RETURN HOME. I DON'T WANT TO LEAVE MY FAMILY.

"We would only be gone for two years. Then, Serafina, we could return and prosper here."

Serafina's husband believes going to America is a way to find work and save money for two years. Serafina helps take care of her large family in Italy. She could send money to them, but she would have to leave everything behind, with no guarantee that she would be able to return. What should she do? Explain the pros and cons of the answer you chose.

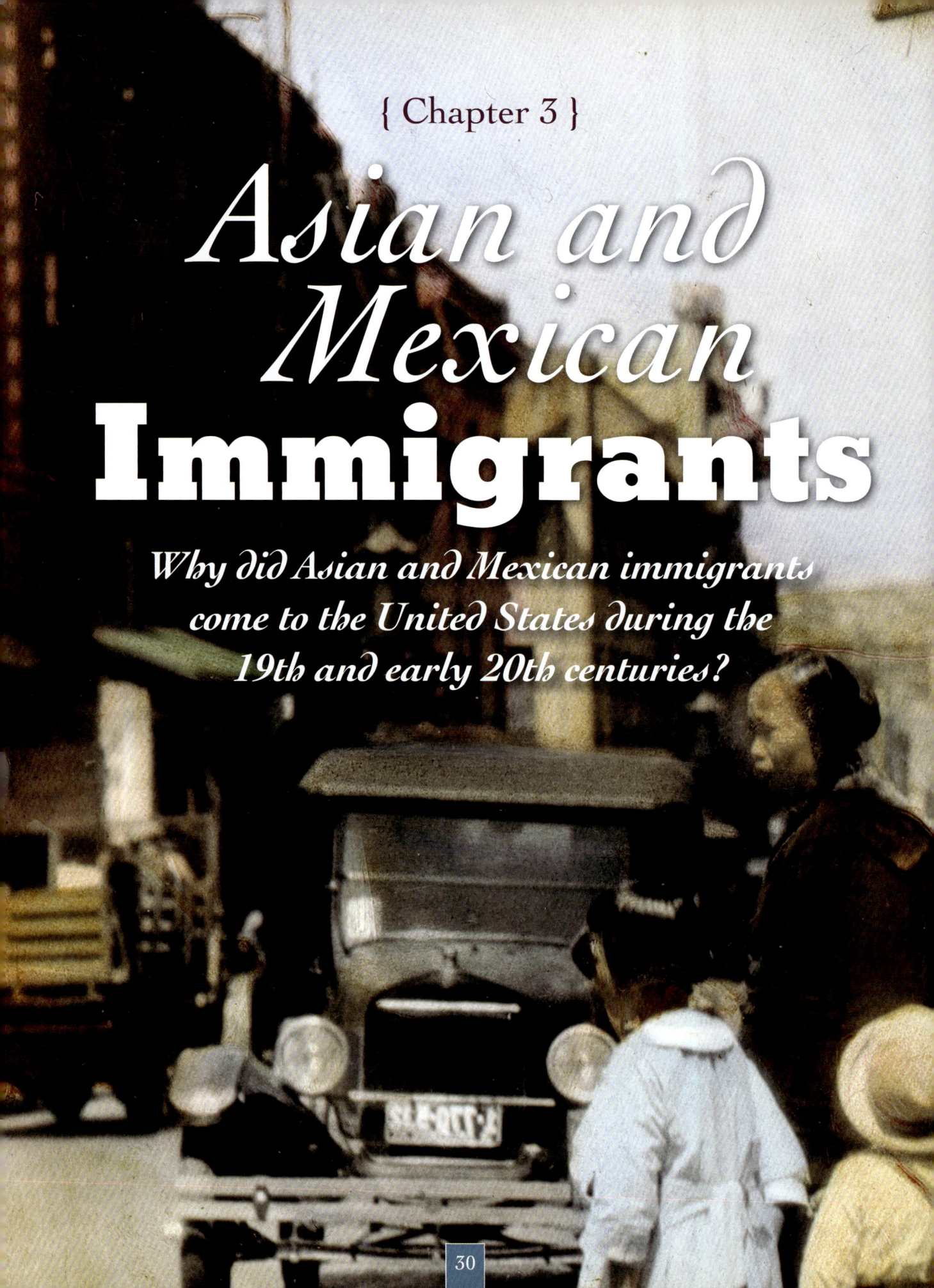

{ Chapter 3 }

Asian and Mexican Immigrants

Why did Asian and Mexican immigrants come to the United States during the 19th and early 20th centuries?

ESSENTIAL VOCABULARY

- Anglo — page 36
- barrio — page 37
- Californio — page 36
- Manifest Destiny — page 35
- mission — page 34
- mutualista — page 37
- presidio — page 34
- visa — page 38

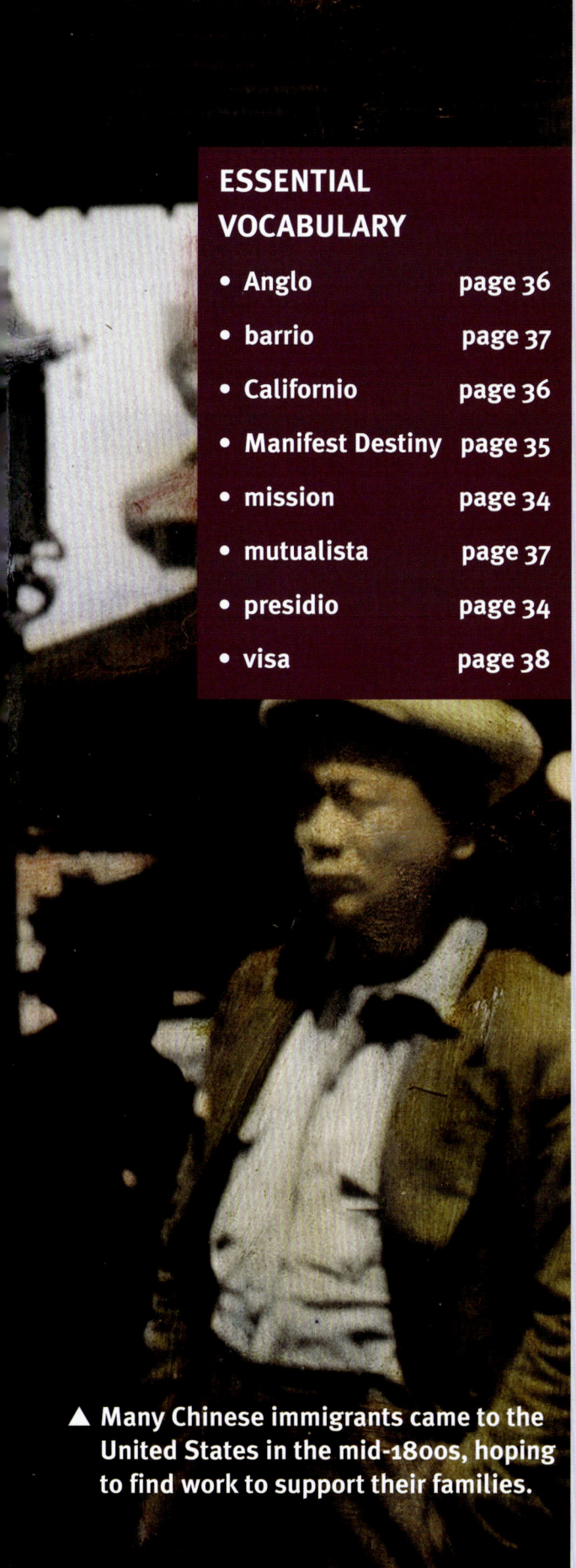

▲ Many Chinese immigrants came to the United States in the mid-1800s, hoping to find work to support their families.

While millions of Europeans immigrated to the United States from 1850 to 1920, immigrants from the east, in Asia, and from the south, in Mexico, also added to the vibrant American tapestry.

Asian Immigration to the United States

During the 1840s, Chinese immigrants crossed the Pacific and arrived in California. Most were men hoping to strike it rich in the California goldfields. What they found in the goldfields, however, was deep discrimination. A special tax was levied on the Chinese by the state of California to make it difficult for them to keep mining. They also faced violence at the hands of American prospectors, or miners. Many Chinese immigrants at this time also came to find work in agriculture and in manufacturing. Many worked in the garment industry.

Many Chinese immigrants eventually left the goldfields, and in the 1850s, thousands went to work on the railroads. During the 1860s, the Union Pacific Railroad and the Central Pacific Railroad were trying to link the Pacific Coast to the Atlantic Coast in a transcontinental railroad. Chinese workers were employed by the Central Pacific to build the western spur. They were paid less than the railroad paid white workers. They also endured enormous hardships laying track through the high Sierra Nevada mountains, blasting tunnels through the thick rock, and continuing to work through harsh winters in order to finish the job. The railroad was finally completed in 1869.

{ Chapter 3 }

When the transcontinental railroad was completed, the Chinese found jobs on other railroads. Because they often were supporting families back in China, or repaying their fare, they were often forced to take whatever jobs they could get and therefore worked for large farm owners looking to harvest their crops at low cost. However, as the number of Chinese laborers increased, anti-Chinese sentiment grew, resulting in rampant discrimination against Chinese immigrants, including a set of laws known as the Chinese Exclusion Acts.

By the mid-1870s, as an economic downturn gripped the United States, jobs became harder to find. White workers resented the fact that Chinese laborers were being employed while some Anglos did not have jobs. In 1877 a race riot broke out in San Francisco, home to many Chinese immigrants who lived in Chinatown. Anti-Chinese sentiment began to grow across the United States, and some political leaders began to talk about the "yellow peril," a negative way of referring to the Chinese.

In 1882, the United States Congress reacted to the resentment expressed by white voters and passed the Chinese Exclusion Act. The law, which was extended in 1892 and 1902, prohibited more Chinese from immigrating to the United States. It also prevented Chinese immigrants already living in the country from becoming citizens.

▼ San Francisco in 1900 had one of the largest populations of Chinese immigrants in the United States.

In 1905, the Asiatic Exclusion League was formed. It pressured the California legislature to pass a law putting Asian children in segregated schools. In 1913, the California Alien Land Law prevented Asian immigrants from owning land. This included Chinese, Korean, and Japanese immigrants.

In the mid-1800s, Japanese had begun immigrating to Hawaii, where they worked picking sugarcane and pineapple. They also became agricultural workers in California. About four hundred thousand people left Japan between 1886 and 1924 to escape economic problems at home.

In large part to deal with the prejudice they found in America, Chinese and Japanese immigrants formed their own communities. For example, San Francisco had a large Chinatown. These immigrants brought new styles of clothing with them, Japanese and Chinese foods, as well as holiday celebrations that broadened American culture. In the decades ahead, other Asian immigrants who helped transform America would join them.

Picture Brides

Japanese immigrants were almost entirely men. Gradually, matchmakers tried to arrange marriages for male immigrants with young women in Japan. Some women were motivated to marry and move to America because their families were poor and they wanted a better life. Others agreed because their parents had already made the arrangements, and they wanted to be obedient daughters. The term "picture brides" arose because the men sent pictures of themselves to Japan for the families of the young women to select husbands for their daughters. Some men sent pictures that misrepresented their actual appearance—in reality, they may have been much older or far less handsome. Often the women were disappointed when they arrived and saw their future husbands, but they consented to the marriages and raised families in Hawaii or on the West Coast of the United States.

{ Chapter 3 }

The Beginnings of Hispanic Immigration

In 1513, a Spanish explorer named Juan Ponce de León landed on the coast of Florida. He was among the first Europeans to set foot in North America.

In 1565, the Spanish established a colony in Florida. During the 1600s and 1700s, they also established settlements in what would become Arizona, New Mexico, Texas, and California. They governed these last four settlements from their capital in Mexico City. The Spanish were drawn to North America by their desire to discover gold and silver. But they also came to convert the indigenous people of the region to Christianity.

In 1718, the Spanish established a settlement at San Antonio, Texas. Similar to others in their North American empire, the settlement included both a **mission** for religious education and a **presidio**, or fort, for protection.

▲ Juan Ponce de León was the first governor of Puerto Rico, and he led the first group of Spaniards to explore Florida.

▼ Established by the Spanish, Santa Fe, New Mexico, is the oldest capital city in North America.

Asian and Mexican Immigrants

Beginning in 1769, the Spanish, led by Father Junípero Serra and a soldier named Gaspar de Portolá, established a series of missions and presidios along the California coast. They stretched for more than five hundred miles northward from San Diego. The road that connected them was called El Camino Real, "the King's Highway."

Only a few hundred Spanish settlers came to California during the 1700s. The settlements in Arizona, New Mexico, and Texas were also thinly populated. During the early 1800s, settlers from the United States began moving into the Spanish empire. By 1825, Stephen Austin had established a settlement in Texas that numbered 2,500 people. The population grew to about twenty thousand in 1830. By then the American settlers, who greatly outnumbered the Spanish in Texas, no longer wanted to live in an empire controlled from Mexico City. In 1836, they declared their independence. After a brief and victorious war against the Mexican government, the region became the independent Lone Star Republic. Then, in 1845, Texas joined the United States as a state.

▲ The Mexican Cession of 1848 added these territories to the United States.

In 1845, the United States went to war with Mexico. U.S. President James Polk wanted to add New Mexico, Arizona, and California to the United States. Polk and many other Americans believed in **Manifest Destiny**. That is, they thought the destiny of the United States was to control the continent from the Atlantic Ocean to the Pacific Ocean. In the Mexican-American War (1845–1848), U.S. forces defeated the armies of Mexico. As a result, in 1848, Mexico surrendered more than half (55 percent) of its land area to the United States—including California, Arizona, New Mexico, Utah, and Nevada—as part of the Mexican Cession.

◀ A series of missions in California, like this one at San Diego, was founded by Father Junípero Serra.

{ Chapter 3 }

▲ Mexican families continued to immigrate to the United States in the late 1800s and early 1900s.

Mexican Americans living in these territories now became citizens of the United States. According to the 1848 Treaty of Guadalupe Hidalgo that ended the Mexican-American War, the lands owned by the Mexicans were supposed to be protected. But this did not happen. In California, for example, the Spanish—known as **Californios**—quickly began to lose their land to **Anglos**—English-speaking white settlers. The Anglos challenged the Californio land grants, which were often very old and not recognized by American courts of law.

In 1848, gold was discovered in California, where thousands of people came hoping to get rich in the goldfields. Approximately fifteen thousand Mexican miners immigrated to California from Mexico by 1850. But the Mexican miners faced discrimination in California. Mexican miners were charged a monthly tax of twenty dollars—a large sum then—to dig in the goldfields. This forced many to leave. Others who paid the tax and stayed often found themselves driven off their claims by Anglo miners, who used violence and intimidation.

▲ Spanish landowners were driven off their estates by Anglos and forced to work for them.

Some of those immigrants became farmworkers, and went to work for Anglos who had taken over Spanish estates. These farmworkers were known as peons, people who planted fruits and vegetables on the vast estates and later harvested them for low wages. But these conditions did not discourage immigrants, who continued to arrive from Mexico to work in California as well as in Arizona, New Mexico, and Texas. Some worked in mines, while others joined crews to build railroads that were beginning to stretch across the Southwest. Nevertheless, the Mexican workers faced the same prejudice as those who lived in California. Anglo miners drove them out of mining jobs. The railroads routinely paid Mexican workers less than Anglos.

In response, Mexican immigrants began to rely on each other for protection. They lived in their own neighborhoods, known as **barrios**, in many towns. These barrios had shops that catered only to Mexican residents. The immigrants also established **mutualistas**, aid societies to help one another. These mutualistas provided loans for immigrants who wanted to set up small businesses in the barrios and schools to educate Mexican children.

Within these communities, Mexican immigrants carried on the cultural traditions that they had known in Mexico. Among these were Mexican foods, like tortillas—thin corn cakes—and chili dishes made of chopped beef, tomatoes, and peppers. The immigrants held fiestas to celebrate holidays and upheld their rich traditions of dance and mariachi folk music. All of these traditions eventually became part of the American culture.

▼ Mexican immigrants worked on the railroads but were paid a lower wage than Anglo workers.

{ Chapter 3 }

Great Mexican Migration, 1900–1930

From 1884 to 1911, Mexico was ruled off and on by a dictator named Porfirio Díaz. President Díaz transformed the Mexican economy, welcoming investment from the United States and Europe. As a result, the railroads expanded, mining operations grew, and wealthy landowners became even richer. But the economic boom did not help average Mexican farmers. They found themselves working for the large landowners at very low wages. In addition, a large increase in population among the Mexican people made jobs difficult to find.

During the first decade of the 20th century, the Mexican economy began to slow down. Opposition to President Díaz had been growing, and he was finally overthrown in a revolution in 1910. Once the revolution was over, however, the opposition groups began to disagree among themselves. Mexico was plunged into a bloody civil war that claimed the lives of more than one million people.

To escape the violence of war and its aftermath, many Mexicans left their homeland and crossed the Rio Grande River, which separated their country from the United States. Then they headed into California, Texas, and other states in the Southwest. Approximately one and a half million Mexicans arrived in the United States from 1900 to 1930. Some crossed the border legally with **visas** permitting them to live in the United States; others came illegally, looking for opportunities in the United States.

Checkpoint
Read More About It

Do research on the U.S. Border Patrol, which started patrolling the Mexican and Canadian borders in the 1920s.

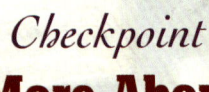
▲ Born in 1878, Doroteo Arango later changed his name to Pancho Villa.

They Made a Difference

Pancho Villa

Pancho Villa was one of the most controversial leaders of the Mexican civil war. Born in 1878, his real name was José Doroteo Arango Arámbula, but he later took the name of a dead outlaw leader named Pancho Villa. Villa was among several rebel leaders who helped overthrow Porfirio Díaz and replaced him with a new president, Francisco I. Madero. But there was soon a falling out among Madero and the rebel leaders. Madero was overthrown in 1913 by General Victoriano Huerta. A brutal dictator, Huerta was himself driven from power by Villa and other leaders who replaced him in 1914 with another president, Venustiano Carranza. Villa later revolted against Carranza, too, and began carrying out raids in Mexico and New Mexico. Many Mexicans regarded Villa as a hero who robbed the rich and provided money to the poor, while others believed he was nothing but a bandit. He was finally assassinated in 1923.

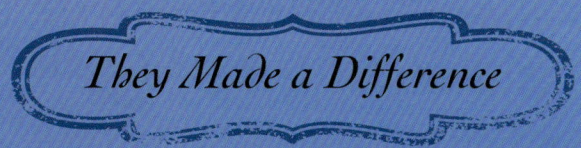

{ Chapter 3 }

In the United States, the Mexican immigrants found jobs at wages higher than they had received in Mexico. Cotton farms and ranches had been expanding in the Southwest, and they needed inexpensive labor to work on them. Many immigrants also headed northward in California, where they were employed to bring in fruit and vegetable harvests. After a harvest was completed, these migrant workers might move to another area to bring in another crop. Some immigrants spent their lives moving from place to place and living in makeshift camps. Others settled down in barrios in major cities, such as Los Angeles, California.

But like Mexican Americans of earlier generations, they faced discrimination. Their children were forced to attend segregated schools, and some restaurants and stores refused to serve them. The steady stream continued to arrive until about 1930, when the United States had plunged into the Great Depression. No new jobs were available; in fact, millions of people were being laid off from work. Farmers and ranchers could now find many more hands to work in their fields, so inexpensive Mexican labor was no longer necessary. As a result, hundreds of thousands of Mexicans returned to Mexico, often with the help of the mutualistas in their barrios. This brought an end, at least for a time, to their mass immigration to the United States.

▼ Economic conditions in the 1930s convinced many Mexican Americans to return to Mexico.

Summing Up

- Spanish settlers began arriving in North America in the 1500s. Many settled in California and the Southwest, which eventually became part of the United States.

- During the 19th century, large numbers of Mexican immigrants crossed the border into the United States, where they worked in the goldfields and on farms and ranches. With them came their rich culture, which changed the social fabric of the United States.

- They were joined by Asian immigrants, especially Chinese and Japanese, who lived primarily in California.

- Chinese workers helped build the railroads.

- Japanese immigrants harvested much of the agricultural produce enjoyed by other Americans.

Putting It All Together

Choose one of the following research activities. Work independently, in pairs, or in small groups. Share your responses with your class, and listen to others present their work.

1. In 1836, Col. Davy Crockett fought against General Santa Anna of Mexico at the famous battle of the Alamo near San Antonio, Texas. Research each side's point of view on this battle for Texan independence from Mexico. How did Santa Anna view the Texans? How did Crockett and the Texans view Santa Anna?

2. Read about the growth of the Mexican American community in Los Angeles in the 1900s. Then create a multimedia presentation that explores this community.

3. Research the building of the transcontinental railroad during the 1860s. Why was the work done by the Chinese laborers often more dangerous and time-consuming than that done by the Union Pacific workers? Find out and write an explanation.

{ Conclusion }

The Great Mosaic

Today, the stories of many American families begin with those ancestors who first immigrated to the United States. There are many factors that drove America's immigrants to its shores. Thanks to photographers like Lewis Hine, we can see what it was like to first arrive at Ellis Island. And thanks to other firsthand accounts, personal narratives, and other primary sources, we can learn about the many varied immigrant experiences that have made the United States "the great American Mosaic" of cultures and identities that it is today.

How to Write a Biography

A biography is the story of someone's life and can range from a few sentences to a volume of books. A biography should describe and analyze the events in a person's life. It should try to find meaning in actions and make arguments about the significance of the person's accomplishments.

Research

1. Choose a person of interest to you to research in depth.
2. Read articles on your subject in magazines, encyclopedias, or online sources.
3. Use this information to make a preliminary outline for your biography.
4. Do additional research in the library, including published biographies of your subject or filmed documentaries.
5. Find examples of songs that your subject wrote or performed, literature that the subject wrote, or art that he or she produced.
6. Write a revised outline based on all of the information that you have collected.
7. Look for an interesting event in the life of the subject that would catch the attention of your readers.

Writing

8. Use this interesting event to begin the biography.
9. Then write the rest of the biography in chronological order.
10. Be sure to integrate the events of the historical period with the life of your subject.
11. Emphasize major themes in your subject's life.
12. Include quotes from what your subject said or wrote or direct quotes from people who knew the subject personally or professionally.

Revising

13. Reread your biography and check facts against the information in your sources.
14. Reread your biography aloud and listen to the sentences. Make sure they are clear and easy to read.
15. Reread your biography a third time and check it for grammar and punctuation.
16. Add any pictures of your subject if these would enhance the biography.

Sample Biography

Albert Einstein was born in Ulm, Germany, on March 14, 1879. Soon after, his family moved to Switzerland. He was a quiet and shy boy, but he was very smart and had a good sense of humor. He loved to solve puzzles and build things.

Einstein did not like school very much but he was very curious about the world—always asking questions and then setting out to find the answers. He was good at math and science, so he trained to be a teacher. In 1901, he graduated from school. When he could not find work as a teacher, he took a job at the Swiss Patent Office, where people patent their ideas and inventions.

While he was at the patent office, and in his spare time, he worked very hard on his own ideas about light and physics. Einstein returned to Berlin, Germany, to teach in 1914. By the 1920s, he had written many books and traveled around the world teaching people about physics. By the 1930s, Einstein's fame had made him a target of the rising fascist Nazi party who began burning his books and denouncing his theories as "Jewish Physics."

▲ **Albert Einstein immigrated to America in 1932.**

In 1931, it became obvious to Einstein that the Nazi threat was growing and his life was in danger. He left Germany in December of 1932 and immigrated to America. He became a physics professor at Princeton University in 1933 and an American citizen in 1940. In the years after World War II, Einstein was a leading figure. Though he was famous all over the world for his ideas, he remained shy all of his life. He spent a lot of time alone, thinking and listening to music. Einstein always appeared to have a clear view of a problem and the determination to solve the problem. He had a special way of working. He visualized, or pictured in his mind, the stages on the way to the solution. This helped him reach his goals.

His ideas and scientific discoveries changed what we know about physics. His well-known books include: *Special Theory of Relativity* (1905), *Relativity* (English translations, 1920 and 1950), *General Theory of Relativity* (1916), and *The Evolution of Physics* (1938). He also wrote books about philosophy and peace. Einstein showed the world what hard work and a strong brain could do. He died on April 18, 1955, in Princeton, New Jersey.

Glossary

Anglo (AN-gloh) *noun* a white American who is not Hispanic (page 36)

anti-Semitism (an-tee-SEH-mih-tih-zum) *noun* the hatred of and prejudice against Jewish people (page 13)

barrio (BAR-ee-oh) *noun* part of a city or town in which many of the residents speak Spanish (page 37)

Californio (ka-lih-FOR-nee-oh) *noun* an original Spanish settler of California (page 36)

census (SEN-sus) *noun* an official survey used to determine the population of a specific place (page 7)

emigrate (EH-mih-grate) *verb* to leave one's home country to settle in another country (page 8)

ghetto (GEH-toh) *noun* a part of a city where minority groups live (page 12)

immigrate (IH-mih-grate) *verb* to arrive in a country in order to live there permanently (page 7)

indentured servant (in-DEN-cherd SER-vunt) *noun* individual required to serve a master for a specific period of time in exchange for passage across the Atlantic (page 8)

intolerance (in-TAH-luh-runs) *noun* unwillingness to accept the opinions, beliefs, or behaviors of other people (page 20)

Manifest Destiny (MA-nih-fest DES-tih-nee) *noun* the theory that the United States was preordained to control North America from the Atlantic Ocean to the Pacific Ocean (page 35)

mission (MIH-shun) *noun* a group or church assigned to spread its faith to a specific area (page 34)

mutualista (moo-too-ah-LEES-tah) *noun* a mutual-aid society established by Mexican immigrants to help other immigrants (page 37)

pogrom (POH-grum) *noun* the organized killing of a group of people (page 20)

presidio (prih-SEE-dee-oh) *noun* a Spanish military fort (page 34)

pull factor (PUL FAK-ter) *noun* a circumstance that persuades people to live in another country (page 8)

push factor (PUSH FAK-ter) *noun* a circumstance that causes people to leave their home country for another place (page 8)

sweatshop (SWET-shahp) *noun* a business where employees work long hours for little money (page 23)

tsar (ZAR) *noun* a Russian emperor or ruler (page 13)

visa (VEE-zuh) *noun* a document giving temporary permission to live in a country (page 38)

Index

Anglo, 32, 36, 37

anti-Semitism, 13, 20, 27

barrio, 37, 40

Californio, 36

census, 7

Ellis Island, 5, 43

emigrate, 8, 10

ghetto, 12

Gold Rush, 10, 36

Great Potato Famine (Great Hunger), 10

Hine, Lewis, 5, 43

immigrate, 7

indentured servant, 8

intolerance, 20

Manifest Destiny, 35

mission, 34, 35

mutualista, 37, 40

pogrom, 20, 21, 27

presidio, 34, 35

pull factor, 8, 10, 13–15

push factor, 8, 10, 13–15

Riis, Jacob, 22–23

slavery, 9

sweatshop, 23

transcontinental railroad, 31–32

Triangle Shirtwaist Company, 25

tsar, 13, 20, 26

visa, 38